The Making

Of

A Champion!

Dr. Frank L. Hammonds

ACKNOWLEDGEMENT

First, I give all glory, honor, and praise to my Lord and Savior, Jesus Christ. Without Him, I am nothing. Every word in this book, every lesson I've learned, and every victory I've experienced is because of His grace, mercy, and faithfulness. He is the true Champion of champions.

To my beloved wife Denine; your unwavering devotion for 44 years of marriage and ministry has been one of God's greatest gifts to me. You've stood by my side in every season encouraging me, praying for me, and laboring in love without seeking recognition. Thank you for being my partner in life and purpose.

To my daughter Towanda; you are my heart and legacy. My prayer is that this book strengthens your walk with Christ and empowers you to fulfill everything God has called you to be. Champions are made in the secret place. Keep your ear to His voice. To my son in law Craig; thank you for loving my daughter and being a man of integrity. I may tease you about turning the backyard into a farm and having tools everywhere like Home Depot exploded in the garage, but I admire your work ethic, creativity, and dedication to our family.

To my late parents—Pastor Rozelle L. Hammonds and Missionary Gladys Hammonds—thank you for building the foundation of faith I now stand on. Daddy, your preaching shaped my calling; Mama, your missionary heart instilled in me compassion and conviction. Though you're no longer here in body, your legacy lives on through me and through this work.

To my brothers—Pastor Rozelle L. Hammonds III, Pastor Richard K. Hammonds, Minister Peter D. Hammonds, and Pastor Marcus J. Hammonds— thank you for standing with me in the ministry and in life. Each of you have been a blessing, a covering, and a source of strength. I am honored to walk this journey with you.

To every member of the churches, I've pastored and every soul I've been privileged to serve—thank you. You've helped shape this message through your love, your prayers, and even your pain. Ministry has never been about perfection—it's about people. I am grateful for every one of you.

To every servant leader, preacher, and believer who feels the weight of the call—this book is for you. May it encourage you in your low places and remind you that God is still making champions, even when it doesn't look like it.

And finally, to those who helped bring this vision to life—editors, designers, and those who prayed me through—thank you. Your support has meant more than words can say.

May this book reach the hearts it was destined for and glorify the God who gave it.

To God be the glory. Always.

INTRODUCTION: The Making Of A Champion

By a Servant Who Has Been Kept by Grace

After more than 50 years of preaching the gospel, shepherding God's people, and walking this journey of faith, I felt led to finally put into writing what the Lord has been teaching me for decades: how champions are made—not in public, but in the hidden places. This book isn't about medals or accolades. It's about spiritual endurance. It's about being forged in the fire, refined by trials, and strengthened through surrender.

The Making of a Champion is a testimony, a reflection, and a roadmap. It's for those who've been called, crushed, and yet continue. It's for leaders who pour out even when they feel empty, and for believers who've been standing in faith even when the evidence hasn't yet shown up.

I didn't write this as a man who has "arrived," but as

one who has been kept. Kept through storms, seasons of lack, personal pain, and leadership pressure. I've watched God build character before He opened doors. I've seen Him promote after seasons of pruning. And I've come to learn that real champions are those who keep saying "yes" to God when it would be easier to quit.

This book is also for my children and grandchildren—especially my daughter who has honored my life with her own. I pray these words give strength to the weary, hope to the discouraged, and direction to those searching for purpose.

Everything in these pages comes back to this truth: you don't become a champion because of your strength—you become one because of His.

May this book point you back to Jesus, the true Champion of our faith.

"But thanks be to God, who gives us the victory through our Lord Jesus Christ." —1 Corinthians 15:57

Table of Contents

THERE'S A WAR GOING ON!

Revelation 12:7– "And there was war in heaven: Michael and his angels fought against the dragon; and the dragon fought and his angels."

In the very beginning, before the foundations of the earth were laid. A war broke out in the most unlikely of places: Heaven. The realm of peace, order, and divine presence became the battlefield for a rebellion. Lucifer, the once-glorious archangel, lifted himself in pride and dared to oppose God. With cunning deception, he rallied a third of the angelic host to his cause. But their rebellion was swiftly crushed.

Michael, the archangel, led God's faithful warriors in a celestial conflict. The battle did not last long. Jesus Himself bore witness to its conclusion: *"I beheld Satan fall like lightning from Heaven" (Luke 10:18).* That fall was not gentle. It

9

was swift, violent, and final. Though the battle was won in Heaven, war did not end; it shifted. Now it is among us.

There is war in the womb. Pregnancy, though a miracle, can be seen as a form of biological warfare. A mother's body must adapt to the presence of another life. Her immune system must not reject it. Hormones shift. Organs reposition. Her body battles to protect and nurture what is growing inside.

There is war in the body. Take cancer, for instance. It is a ruthless invader. It is a disease where cells mutate, divide uncontrollably, and destroy healthy tissues. Normally, white blood cells patrol and defend, fighting off infections and foreign bodies. Red blood cells carry life-giving oxygen to the body's tissues. But when these systems malfunction, when the balance is broken, the body turns on itself. The result?

Chaos. Pain. War within.

There's also war in the mind. Anxiety, depression, and confusion are all unseen battles that rage daily in the hearts and thoughts of many. The mind becomes a battlefield, and the enemy fights with lies, fear, and distraction. But God has not left us defenseless. "Let this mind be in you, which was also in Christ Jesus" (Philippians 2:5).

There is spiritual warfare. Ephesians 6:12 reminds us: *"For we wrestle not against flesh and blood, but against principalities, against powers, against the rulers of the darkness of this world…"* This war is not physical. It is spiritual. It is waged in prayer, faith, and obedience.

Just as God commanded Joshua to be strong and courageous (Joshua 1:7), so He commands us. Joshua was told to obey the Word and not turn to the right or the left. Victory was promised.

"There shall not any man be able to stand before thee all the days of thy life…" (Joshua 1:5).

Yes, there are wars to be fought. Battles to be won. But we do not fight alone. Heaven fights with us. The same God who cast Satan down empowers us to stand. Whether in the body, the mind, or the spirit, we fight not only for victory, but from victory.

From Genesis to Revelation, and from ancient history to today's headlines, life is marked by battles. Some we see. Some we feel. Some rage silently within. There are both natural and spiritual wars being fought every day.

But God's promise remains sure. He told Joshua, *"As I was with Moses, so shall I be with you. No man shall be able to stand before you all the days of your life"* *(Joshua 1:5)*. That promise is still alive for us today. You are not alone in the war. God is with you.

Even in the natural realm, history testifies. The United States alone has seen at least eleven major wars, including the Civil War in a fight to end the bondage of slavery. Every war had a cause, a cost, and a victor. But the wars we fight in the spirit carry eternal weight.

<u>Here are just a few of the spiritual battles we face:</u>

1. **The war between the flesh and the Spirit**: *"For the flesh lusteth against the Spirit, and the Spirit against the flesh…" (Galatians 5:17).* Every day, we must choose who leads. The carnal or the spiritual.

2. **The war in the mind**: Thoughts of fear, doubt, shame, and defeat try to take root. But *"be transformed by the renewing of your mind" (Romans 12:2).*

3. **The war in the body**: Sickness, fatigue,

and attacks on your health may come, but God is still Jehovah Rapha, your Healer.

4. **The war between righteousness and unrighteousness**: Light and darkness can't coexist. You must choose to stand for truth.

5. **The war between angels and demons**: Even now, angels fight on your behalf. There are things shifting in the unseen realm.

6. **The war between sin and salvation**: There's a daily pull, but Jesus has already paid the price. Choose life.

"The weapons of our warfare are not carnal, but mighty through God to the pulling down of strongholds" (2 Corinthians 10:4). You can't win these battles with fists or guns but only with faith, prayer, the Word, and the blood of Jesus.

The Bible declares, "There was war in Heaven"

(Revelation 12:7). Satan tried to overthrow the throne of God. But the war wasn't just about rebellion, it was about praise. Lucifer wanted the worship that belongs to God alone. Even now, there's a war for your praise. The enemy knows that if he can steal your praise, he can weaken your spirit. But don't let him.

Remember the walls of Jericho? They fell when the people marched around seven times and lifted a SHABACH with a loud, triumphant praise! (Joshua 6)

So even when it gets hard...

1. Keep Fighting!
2. Keep Believing!
3. Keep Trusting!
4. Keep Standing!
5. Keep Holding On!

Victory is yours not because of your strength, but because God is with you in the war.

In the womb of Rebekah, even before birth, a war was raging. Two children struggled within her. Esau and Jacob. These represent two nations, two destinies, two opposing forces (Genesis 25:22-23). This was not just a family matter; it was a prophetic war, a preview of the spiritual conflicts that would unfold throughout history.

Today, we still face battles on every side. There is a war against the Devil, who prowls like a roaring lion, seeking whom he may devour. There is a war against sin, which seeks to enslave us. There is a war against death, but thanks be to God, who gives us victory through Jesus Christ. There is even a war against sickness, as the enemy attacks the body to weaken faith and purpose.

The Devil has declared war on the saints of the Most High. He is fighting:

1. Over your soul

2. Over your finances

3. Over your health

4. Over your children

5. Over your peace of mind

Just as King Jehoshaphat faced three armies at once (2 Chronicles 20), you may feel surrounded. But remember the battle is not yours, it is the Lord's. Victory is assured for those who trust in Him.

THE FIGHT IS ON

2 Timothy 4:7-8— *"I have fought a good fight, I have finished my course, I have kept the faith: Henceforth there is laid up for me a crown of righteousness, which the Lord, the righteous judge, shall give me at that day: and not to me only, but unto all them also that love his appearing."*

The Apostle Paul was nearing the end of his earthly journey. Writing to Timothy, his spiritual son, he wasn't boasting, but he was testifying. He had *fought a good fight*. He had endured trials, persecutions, betrayals, shipwrecks, beatings, and more, yet he held on. He didn't give up. He didn't back down. He didn't lose faith.

Paul's declaration wasn't just about surviving battles; it was about winning them. You can fight and still lose. You can struggle and still be defeated. But when you've fought a good fight, it means you stood firm, kept the faith, and emerged victorious. A good fight is a fight that ends in triumph.

Today, we are living in a time where the people of God must rise up and fight a good fight. Not just any fight. Not against each other. Paul didn't say, "I fought the saints." He said, "I fought a good fight." But too often in the Body of Christ, we see saints fighting saints, preachers tearing down preachers, and churches competing instead of collaborating. That's the wrong fight.

We're not called to fight one another; we're called to fight the enemy. There is one adversary, and his name is Satan. He comes to steal, kill, and destroy. He launches attacks against your mind, your home, your finances, your children, your peace, and your purpose. So, you must make up your mind: "This test, this trial, this attack I will not let it defeat me!"

You've got to plant your feet and say it with fire:

"Devil, the fight is on!"

When you say *"The fight is on,"* you are saying:

1. I am not giving up!

2. I am not giving in!

3. I will not quit!

4. I will not buckle!

5. I will not go under!

6. I am not afraid!

You are telling the devil:

Enough is enough.

This will be a knock-down, drag-out war, and I'm not backing down.

But the good news is, we are not defenseless.

God has given us weapons. Spiritual weapons. Mighty weapons.

2 Corinthians 10:4-5 says:

"For the weapons of our warfare are not carnal, but mighty through God to the pulling down of strongholds; Casting down imaginations, and every high thing that exalteth itself against the knowledge of God..."

That means we don't fight with fists or fury, we fight with truth, prayer, faith, the Word, the blood of Jesus, and the name above every name!

We fight by casting down lies and every false thought that tries to rise above what God has said. Every whisper that says, *"You're not enough. You won't make it. God has forgotten you."*
We arrest those thoughts and bring them into obedience to Christ.

We remind ourselves:

"I am more than a conqueror!" (Romans 8:37)

"No weapon formed against me shall prosper!" (Isaiah 54:17)

"Greater is He that is in me than he that is in the world!" (1 John 4:4)

This is not the time to be timid.

This is not the time to fold under pressure.

This is the time to stand up and fight.

Let the devil know:

"You touched the wrong one this time!"

"I might be tired, but I'm still standing!"

"I may be weeping, but joy is coming in the morning!"

"I've got a crown waiting on me, and I will not be denied!"

Because after the fight, there is a reward.

Paul said, *"Henceforth there is laid up for me a crown*

of righteousness..."

And not just for him, but for all who love His appearance.

Fight now, knowing there's a crown later.

Endure now, knowing there's glory after this.

Let this be your war cry:

1. I will fight until I finish!

2. I will finish and keep the faith!

3. And when it's all said and done, I will receive my crown!

Matthew 11:12

"And from the days of John the Baptist until now the kingdom of heaven suffereth violence, and the violent take it by force."

Ephesians 6:11-12

"Put on the whole armour of God, that ye may be able to stand against the wiles of the devil.

For we wrestle not against flesh and blood, but against principalities, against powers, against the rulers of the darkness of this world, against spiritual wickedness in high places."

The Word of God doesn't sugarcoat it. This walk of faith is not passive. It's not for the faint of heart. It is war. Spiritual war. It takes force, faith, and focus to live for God in a world filled with darkness, deception, and demonic interference.

In Matthew 11:12, Jesus points out that the Kingdom of Heaven suffers violence, and the violent take it by force. What does that mean? It means this Kingdom life, this righteous, holy, fruitful life, will cost you something. You don't drift into it. You fight for it. You take it. The Kingdom is not seized by casual believers. It's claimed by those who are willing to wage war in the Spirit and fight the good fight of faith.

Fighting Words Matter

Remember back in school? The moment someone said, *"Your mama,"* you knew a fight was coming. Why? Because those were fighting words. Kids didn't tolerate disrespect toward their mother, someone they loved and honored. The moment those words were uttered, the heart kicked in. Passion rose. Fists clenched. Someone was ready to throw down.

Now take that same intensity, and ask yourself: Are you ready to fight for your faith like that? Are you ready to defend your calling, your family, your peace, your anointing?

The devil has launched an attack:

1. Against your finances

2. Against your peace of mind

3. Against your sanity

4. Against your joy

5. Against your marriage

6. Against your children

7. Against your calling

But instead of letting discouragement sit on your chest like a heavy weight, instead of throwing in the towel, it's time to stand up and say:

Devil, the fight is ON!

It's Time to Go to War

When the enemy comes in like a flood, the Bible says the Spirit of the Lord will lift up a standard against him (Isaiah 59:19). But that standard must rise through you. That means taking spiritual warfare seriously. That means suiting up and showing up.

Ephesians 6:11 commands us to *"Put on the whole armour of God..."* Why? Because we are wrestling. Not against people. Not against your boss, your spouse, or your neighbor, but against *"principalities... powers... the rulers of darkness... spiritual wickedness in high places."* That's not casual stuff. That's deep warfare. That's a demonic hierarchy. And it requires spiritual strength and strategy.

So, what do you do when the enemy attacks?

You don't retreat - you reload.

You don't fold - you fight.

You don't complain - you combat.

Declare It Loud: "Devil, The Fight Is On!"

When the devil pushes, you push back. Don't

push back with your feelings, you push back with your faith.

Tell the devil:

"I'm going to increase my prayer time!"

"I'm going to fast!"

"I'm going to read my Bible!"

"I'm going to lay hands on the sick and see them recover!"

"I'm going to prophesy and declare victory over my household!"

"I'm going to pray in the Spirit!"

You want a fight, devil?

You've got one.

I'm stepping up my:

1. Faith

2. Focus

3. Fire

4. Fight

I'm casting down every imagination.

I'm pulling down every stronghold.

I'm tearing down every lie.

I'm suiting up in the armor of God.

I'm picking up my shield of faith and my sword of the Spirit.

And I will not be moved!

The Bible is full of fighting language. There's fighting words everywhere:

1. Weapons - for battle

2. Warfare - strategic and intentional

3. Violence - not passive surrender

4. Armor - for protection

5. Strongholds- that need to be broken

6. Force - applied to claim victory

None of these words suggests comfort. They suggest combat, but we are not alone in the fight. God has equipped us, empowered us, and gone before us.

Fight for What Matters

Some things are worth fighting for:

1. Fight for your deliverance!

2. Fight for your freedom!

3. Fight for your marriage!

4. Fight for your children!

5. Fight for your healing!

6. Fight for your joy!

7. Fight for your salvation!

8. Fight for your breakthrough!

9. Fight for your peace!

10. Fight for your promise!

And when you feel weak, remember:

"Let the weak say, I am strong." (Joel 3:10)

The War Has Already Been Won

Here's the best part: The fight may be on, but the victory is already yours. You're not fighting for victory; you're fighting from victory. Jesus already defeated death, hell, and the grave. The blood has already been shed. The tomb is already empty. The keys of death and hell are already in His hands.

Now, your job is to enforce that victory in your life.

"Submit yourselves therefore to God. Resist the devil, and he will flee from you." (James 4:7)

So yes, the battle is real.

But so is your God.

So is your authority.

So is your anointing.

The fight is on and you've been chosen to win.

1. Put on your armor.

2. Grab your weapons.

3. Lift up your voice.

4. Stand in your authority.

5. Call on the name of Jesus.

6. And fight like someone who already knows how the story ends.

You are not going under. You are going over.

You are not being defeated. You are already delivered.

You are not quitting. You are conquering.

Why? Because the FIGHT IS ON and GOD IS WITH YOU.

THE POWER OF THE PROPHETIC WORD!

Ezekiel 37:1–10– *"The hand of the Lord was upon me, and carried me out in the spirit of the Lord, and set me down in the midst of the valley which was full of bones..."*

The prophet Ezekiel was not taken to a mountaintop. He was not placed in a garden. He wasn't brought into a palace or a peaceful place. He was carried by the Spirit of the Lord into a valley full of bones, not just bones, but bones that were very dry.

This wasn't just a symbolic image of death. It was a prophetic message about hope in hopeless places, restoration where decay had ruled, and revival through the spoken Word of God. It was God's visual sermon to Israel and a powerful message for us today.

For years, many have preached on the *dry bones in the valley*, and the emphasis has often been on the *dryness*, the *death*, or the *despair*. But there's more to this prophetic vision than just bones lying on the valley floor.

Yes, the bones represent something that once lived, but has now died. God's message to Ezekiel was not about mourning what was lost. It was about declaring what could live again.

The dry bones in the valley symbolized the house of Israel, which was scattered, broken, spiritually dead, and cut off from hope. They had lost their identity, their power, and their connection to the God who had called them out of Egypt. Yet, even in that death-like state, God had not forgotten them.

And what did God do? He didn't send an army.

He didn't send water. He didn't even send angels.

He sent a word.

"Prophesy to These Bones"

God asked Ezekiel a question: *"Son of man, can these bones live?"* And the prophet, with reverent humility, answered: *"O Lord God, You know."*

Then came the command:

"Prophesy to these bones, and say to them, 'O dry bones, hear the word of the Lord!'"

This was not a request. It was a divine charge. God was demonstrating to Ezekiel and to us the power of the prophetic word.

God didn't say to Ezekiel, "Tell Me what you see." He said, "Speak what I tell you."

When you declare what God says, you release the

power of divine transformation.

Prophecy brings alignment.

Prophecy awakens purpose.

Prophecy revives what looks dead.

Bones don't respond to logic. Dryness doesn't yield to emotion. Death doesn't retreat just because you cry. But when you speak what God says, everything changes.

God showed Ezekiel the process. Restoration doesn't always come all at once. Sometimes there's a noise before there's a miracle. Sometimes there's a shaking before there's standing. Sometimes structure comes before spirit. Don't stop prophesying just because it looks incomplete. Keep speaking.

God said:

"Prophesy to the wind. Say to the breath: Come from the four winds, O breath, and breathe upon these slain, that they may live."

Bones represent what once was. They speak of deterioration, of what used to be full of life, movement, and purpose. When all that remains is bones, we are staring at the aftermath of death. A life that was, a promise that seemed to pass, a vision that dried up.

But bones also represent structure. The human body consists of muscles, flesh, and skin, yet none of these can hold form without bones. Bones are the framework, the foundation that gives strength, stability, and support. Without bones, the body collapses.

Another word for bones is skeleton, which literally means the remains or the outline of what once existed. The skeleton is the memory of a person or a purpose. It is the infrastructure left behind after life has left. And herein lies the revelation: when God tells the prophet Ezekiel to prophesy to the bones, He's not just commanding him to speak life, He's commanding him to speak structure back into broken things.

God told Ezekiel:

"Prophesy to these bones, and say unto them, O ye dry bones, hear the word of the Lord." (Ezekiel 37:4)

This was not a poetic suggestion. This was a divine order to speak to the forgotten, the dried out, the left behind, the scattered. And it reveals a powerful truth: the prophetic word is creative. It doesn't just confirm what exists, it brings into existence what isn't there yet.

Romans 4:17 echoes this:

"...even God, who quickeneth the dead, and calleth those things which be not as though they were."

This isn't just faith, this is prophetic faith. This is God-kind of faith. It is seeing through spiritual eyes and speaking what heaven sees, even when the earth shows the opposite.

When we say "let there be," we are stepping into our divine authority. That's what God did in Genesis 1:3 when He said, *"Let there be light,"* even though darkness covered the earth. There was no light, but His word created light. That's the power of prophetic speech.

When God told Ezekiel to prophesy, it wasn't about wishful thinking. It was a command to create, to reconstruct, and to restore what had been lost. The prophetic word fills in the skeleton. It puts flesh on the frame. It covers the structure with life again.

As Ezekiel obeyed and prophesied, something happened:

1. There was a noise

2. Then a shaking

3. Then the bones came together

4. Then sinew and flesh appeared

5. Then the skin covered the bodies

6. But there was still no breath

So, God told him to prophesy again — this time to the wind.

"Prophesy to the wind... and say, Thus saith the Lord GOD; Come from the four winds, O breath, and breathe upon these slain, that they may live." (Ezekiel 37:9)

The prophetic word didn't just bring structure, it brought spirit. The wind came. Breath entered. And the bones stood up, not just as people, but as an exceedingly great army.

That's the power of the prophetic word. It doesn't just revive what was dead, it repositions it for battle.

In 2 Kings 7:1, There was a famine in Samaria, people were starving, and the situation was grim. But the prophet Elisha opens his mouth and declares:

"Hear ye the word of the Lord; Thus saith the LORD, Tomorrow about this time shall a measure of fine flour be sold for a shekel..."

This is what the prophetic word does: it speaks tomorrow into today.

While the people were focusing on their present lack, Elisha was prophesying future provision. The prophetic does not speak based on what is seen; it speaks based on what God says is coming. The famine didn't move the word; the word moved the famine.

We are often so consumed with what we see now that we forget what God is saying next. But the prophetic word declares, *"Don't focus on the valley, prophesy to it!"* Don't describe the dryness; instead, declare the rain.

Everything about God is prophetic. From Genesis to Revelation, He speaks before He performs. He declares before He manifests. He shows the end from the beginning.

When God sent Jesus, it was prophetic from the beginning:

"And she shall bring forth a son, and thou shalt call his name JESUS: for he shall save his people from their sins." (Matthew 1:21)

The plan of redemption wasn't initiated at the

cross; it was spoken before the foundation of the world.

Yes, the devil was defeated at the cross. Yes, he was overcome by the blood. But long before Jesus ever died, the prophetic word declared His victory. The Word made flesh had already won.

So yes, the devil was defeated by the prophetic decree of heaven, long before Calvary unfolded.

Your Mouth Holds Power

Now it's our turn. We must prophesy:

1. To our families

2. To our nations

3. To our dry bones

4. To our purpose

5. To our generation

Prophesy victory into your finances.

Prophesy healing into your body.

Prophesy restoration over your children.

Prophesy life where there's been loss.

Because the moment you speak prophetically, things begin to shift in the realm of the spirit. The change may not be visible immediately in the natural, but it is complete in heaven.

Bones may lie scattered in the valley. Structures may be incomplete. Hope may feel lost. But the power of the prophetic word brings it all back together.

What is your valley today?

What skeletons are you looking at?

Open your mouth and prophesy.

Dry bones live again.

Dead dreams rise again.

Empty places can be filled again.

The wind of God can breathe again.

Let the prophetic word create. Let it fill. Let it quicken.

The hand of the Lord is upon you, and when you speak what He says, everything must change.

In Genesis 3:14–15, God delivers a powerful judgment upon the serpent after the fall of man. The serpent is cursed above all animals and condemned to crawl on its belly, symbolizing ultimate humiliation and defeat. But verse 15 contains the first prophetic promise of redemption.

God says, *"I will put enmity between thee and the woman and between thy seed and her seed."* This foretells a spiritual war between Satan and humanity, but more specifically, between Satan's offspring. The evil and rebellious and the coming Seed of the woman, Jesus Christ.

The prophetic word continues: *"It shall bruise thy head, and thou shalt bruise his heel."* Satan may strike at Christ's heel through suffering and the cross, but Christ will crush Satan's head, symbolizing total victory. This was not just judgment. It was a prophetic declaration of Jesus' triumph over sin and Satan.

I WILL NOT BACK DOWN IF GOD IS BACKING ME UP!

Isaiah 54:17— *"No weapon that is formed against thee shall prosper; and every tongue that shall rise against thee in judgment thou shalt condemn. This is the heritage of the servants of the LORD, and their righteousness is of me, saith the LORD."*

When God is on your side, you don't have to fear what's against you. You don't have to back down, bow out, or break apart. You can stand boldly, knowing the Almighty is backing you up!

The devil will come with weapons of sickness, disease, betrayal, disappointment, lies, persecution, and suffering. But the Word says "no weapon formed shall prosper." The enemy might *form* it, but God won't let it *win*.

Moses stood in front of the Red Sea with

Pharaoh's army chasing him from behind. He didn't run, he didn't retreat, he stood still, because he knew God had his back. When the Israelites panicked, Moses lifted his staff. The sea opened. Why? Because God was backing him up.

Jehoshaphat didn't panic when three massive armies gathered to crush him. He sought the Lord. And God responded by telling him the battle was not his, but the Lord's. When Jehoshaphat praised, God confused the enemy, and they destroyed themselves. Why? Because God had his back.

David faced lions and bears as a shepherd boy, and later, the giant Goliath. He didn't shrink back. He ran *toward* the battlefield, declaring, *"The Lord who delivered me from the lion and the bear will deliver me from this Philistine!"* David knew one thing: if God is backing me up, I don't need to back down.

"What shall we then say to these things? If God be for us, who can be against us?" Romans 8:31

If God is for you, then the outcome has already been decided. You may go through fire, but you won't be burned. You may go through deep waters, but you won't drown. You may face weapons, but they won't prosper.

The only reason you're still standing is because God's been backing you up. Some of the things you made it through others would've collapsed under. But not you. Why? Because the hand of the Lord has been holding you up.

Look at Israel, one of the smallest nations on the planet, about the size of Idaho. Yet despite being outnumbered and surrounded by enemies, no one can destroy them. Why? Because God is backing them up. That same God is your defender.

When the children of Ammon, Moab, and Mount Seir came against Israel, it wasn't just one or two armies, but 31 armies came against them. However, Israel stood still. They didn't run or retreat because God had their back.

Even the prophet Elijah, after calling down fire from heaven and defeating 450 prophets of Baal, collapsed in fear when Jezebel threatened his life. After a spiritual high, he hit an emotional low. He sat under a juniper tree, depressed, and said, *"Lord, I'm the only one left."*

But God corrected him. He said, *"No, Elijah, I've got 7,000 others who haven't bowed to Baal."* In other words: *"You're not alone. You're not forsaken. You're not the only one. I've still got your back."*

So, what do you do when pressure hits?

You don't give up.

You don't quit.

You don't stop.

You don't throw in the towel.

You don't lose heart.

You don't waver.

You don't fall apart.

You don't back down.

Because the same God who backed up Moses, David, Jehoshaphat, and Elijah is backing you up, too.

You Can Make It.

Through the:

1. Trial and Trouble

2. Pain and Misery

3. Disappointment and Hurt

4. Testing and Temptation

5. Struggle and Stress

6. Sickness and Disease

7. Death and Devastation

You can make it. Why? Because God is your support, your covering, your strength, your fortress, your backup!

God's got your back!

Even when you've failed. Even when you've missed the mark. Even when people wrote you off.

In John 8:7, the religious leaders brought a woman caught in adultery to Jesus, ready to stone her. But Jesus stooped down and wrote in the sand. When they demanded a response, He said, *"He that is without sin among you, let him cast the first stone."*

One by one, her accusers dropped their stones

and walked away.

Jesus turned to the woman and asked, *"Where are your accusers?"* And she said, *"There are none, Lord."*

Then He said, *"Neither do I condemn thee. Go and sin no more."*

Even in her lowest moment, God was backing her up.

Not because she was righteous, but because He is merciful. When everyone else wants to stone you, Jesus will stand for you. Even when you're guilty, His grace will cover you. His backing doesn't depend on your perfection; it's anchored in His faithfulness.

You don't have to back down from the:

1. Devil

2. Disease

3. Debt

4. Depression

5. Discouragement

6. Divorce

7. Doubt

If God is backing you up, stand tall.

He's fighting your battles. He's covering your blind spots. He's defending your name. He's lifting your head.

Make this your declaration:

"I will not back down if God is backing me up!"

And when it gets hard, remember: He who started the work in you is faithful to finish it.

You're not alone. You're not forsaken. You're not forgotten.

You're backed by heaven. And that means you're not backing down.

THE NIGHT IS OVER

Psalm 30:5– *"For his anger endureth but a moment; in his favour is life: weeping may endure for a night, but joy cometh in the morning."*

God has been dealing with me deeply about this scripture. The words of the psalmist David are not just poetic, they are prophetic truths born from pain, experience, and divine revelation. When David speaks of weeping enduring for a night, he knows what it's like to live through the night seasons of life.

David wasn't a man speaking from comfort; he was a man familiar with sorrow. This is the same David who said, *"Encourage yourself in the Lord."* Why? Because sometimes no one else will. Sometimes the night is so long, the pain so deep, the rejection so heavy, that encouragement must come from within from your spirit communing with God.

David went through betrayal, heartbreak, moral failure, and unimaginable grief. He lost a child. His best friends turned on him. His own son tried to overthrow him. If anyone could speak with authority about trials, suffering, and darkness it was King David.

When we speak of "the night," we're not just talking about the setting of the sun. We're talking about a season, a period in life marked by suffering, pain, loss, discouragement, and despair. Night is a figure of speech for the times you feel like God is silent, your prayers bounce back, and nothing makes sense.

By definition, night is a time of darkness, gloom, and silence. It represents loneliness, depression, and the absence of clarity. It's the place where hope seems delayed and tears become your closest companion.

"Jesus said, 'We must work the works of Him who sent Me while it is day; the night is coming when no one can work.' John 9:4

Jesus Himself warned that the night is coming, and when it comes, it affects everything. Night is symbolic of a time when clarity is gone, vision is blurred, and opportunities seem out of reach. Night seasons are real, and every believer will walk through one. But the good news is: the night doesn't last forever, and your morning is on the way!

Night seasons are painful. They are the moments when you can't see your next step, when fear whispers louder than faith, and when even prayer feels like a whisper into the void. When you're in the dark, nothing looks right.

Everything feels uncertain. The devil tries to convince you that the night will never end. But he is a liar.

"Let your light so shine before men, that they may see your good works and glorify your Father in heaven." Matthew 5:16

When Jesus tells us to let our light shine, it's not just about being visible; it's about being effective in dark places. Where there is light, darkness has to flee. That's why hell is full of darkness, because there is no presence of God there. In contrast, where God is, there is light, there is clarity, there is hope.

Have you noticed that when people are up to no good, they prefer the night? That's not just literal, it's spiritual. Darkness allows sin to hide, shame to operate, and guilt to grow. Even the places where people go to indulge in the flesh are named after the night: *nightclubs, dark rooms, midnight specials.* But God is calling His people out of the night and into the light of His glory!

"Yea, though I walk through the valley of the shadow of death, I will fear no evil: for thou art with me." Psalm 23:4.

Many of you are walking through your night right now. You've smiled in public but cried in private. You've quoted scriptures out loud, but inside, you're wondering when your season will shift. You're not alone. You are not weak, you're walking through a valley, and God is walking with you.

"If thou faint in the day of adversity, thy strength is small." Proverbs 24:10.

Yes, adversity comes, but it is not meant to destroy you. It is meant to reveal the strength that lies within you. If you don't give up in night, you'll rejoice in the morning. Night is a test of faith, a measure of endurance, and a time of pruning.

That's why Jesus prayed before the break of day. He understood that if you don't command your morning in prayer, your day will be shaped by the residue of your night.

"And at midnight Paul and Silas prayed, and sang praises unto God: and the prisoners heard them." Acts 16:25

Paul and Silas were beaten and imprisoned, locked in the deepest part of the jail. Yet at midnight the darkest part of the night they did what few do: they praised. They didn't panic, they didn't curse, they didn't complain, they prayed and worshiped. And suddenly, the earth shook and the prison doors flew open.

Praise is your weapon in the night. Worship is

your breakthrough key. When the night tries to swallow your joy, open your mouth and declare the goodness of God anyway.

Examples of Those Who Endured the Night

1. Moses spent 40 years in the wilderness. It was a season of isolation and waiting, but God was preparing him to lead a nation.

2. Elijah sat under a juniper tree, overwhelmed and depressed after a mighty victory. He said, *"Lord, take my life."* That was his night season, but God still had more work for him to do.

3. Stephen, full of the Holy Spirit, preached the gospel and was stoned to death, but before he died, he saw heaven open. The night of martyrdom was followed by the vision of glory.

4. The disciples were in the middle of a raging sea, afraid for their lives, but Jesus walked to them in the storm, proving He controls the night too.

5. Jesus Himself endured the darkest night at the cross when He cried, *"My God, my God, why have you forsaken me?"* The Savior of the world was not exempt from night, but He didn't stay there. He rose with power.

6. Peter denied Jesus three times. A personal night of failure and shame. But God restored him and used him to preach with fire at Pentecost.

7. John was isolated on the isle of Patmos. He was exiled, alone, and forgotten. But it was there, in that night season, that he received the Revelation of Jesus Christ.

Night seasons do not last forever. They are temporary tunnels, not permanent graves. The light is breaking through. Joy is returning. Strength is rising. Hope is coming alive.

This is your season of transition out of darkness and into light, out of sorrow and into rejoicing, out of confusion and into clarity. God is declaring over your life:

So, rise up. Shake off the residue of despair. Stand in the confidence that God has kept you, grown you, and refined you in the night, and now He is bringing you into the morning.

"Weeping may endure for a night, but joy comes in the morning."

Get ready, your morning has come. Your joy is here. Your night is over.

IT'S ONLY TEMPORARY

Psalm 30:5– *"his anger endureth but a moment; in his favour is life: weeping may endure for a night, but joy cometh in the morning."*

One translation reads: *"In the evening, weeping may lodge for the night, but in the morning, there is a shout of joy!"* The Moffatt translation puts it this way: *"Tears may visit us at night, but in the morning, there are shouts of joy!"*

These translations all carry the same thunderous message: trouble doesn't always last. The hardship is not permanent. The season of sorrow is not your final chapter. It's only temporary!

When the night seems long and the darkness thick, when you can't see your way and every prayer seems unanswered, you must speak to your own soul:

"This is not the end. This is only temporary." *"This is the day which the Lord has made; we will rejoice and be glad in it." Psalms 118:24.*

Daybreak is always a sign of a breakthrough. Every sunrise reminds us that no matter how long the night was, it cannot stop the coming of a new day. Morning is God's faithful way of saying, *"I'm not finished yet."*

The devil wants to convince you that your current situation is permanent and that the grief you feel will never lift, that the depression will always cloud your mind, that the fear and loss you're facing will define your destiny. But the devil is a liar.

He wants to keep you:

1. Full of sorrow

2. Sinking in grief

3. Weighed down in despair

4. Locked in heartache

5. Lost in hopelessness

6. Surrounded by fear

7. Trapped in depression

But you need to declare over your own life:

"What I'm going through, what I'm feeling, what I'm facing, it's only temporary!"

The Meaning of Temporary

The word temporary means something that:

1. Lasts for a limited time

2. Is not permanent

3. Is seasonal

4. Is subject to change

5. Is short-term

The Bible may not use the English word *temporary* often, but the closest biblical word is temporal found in 2 Corinthians 4:18:

"While we look not at the things which are seen, but at the things which are not seen: for the things which are seen are temporal; but the things which are not seen are eternal."

One translation says: *"The visible things are temporary."*

In other words, everything you're seeing right now, the bills, the stress, the sickness, the betrayal. It's not forever. It's for a moment. It's subject to change.

The Greek word used for *temporal* is "proskairos", meaning *"for an occasion only, for a while, enduring for a season."* That means your storm has a season, and every season has an expiration date.

Job's Temporary Suffering

Think of Job, a man who went through almost unimaginable suffering. He lost:

1. His children

2. His health

3. His wealth

4. His peace

5. His friends

He sat in ashes, scraping boils off his skin, while even his wife said, *"Curse God and die."*

But even that suffering was temporary. Scholars say that Job's entire trial lasted about nine months.

Nine months. What does that sound like to you?

A pregnancy.

That's not just a coincidence. That's divine symbolism. Job's suffering was producing something. His pain was birthing something greater. What you're carrying — your anointing, your testimony, your ministry, your next season is being formed in the dark.

Some labor comes with pain, but pain has a purpose.

And when the time was right, God restored Job, not just to where he had been, but double what he had lost. His weeping endured for a night, but joy exploded in the morning.

As Elder Jimmy (Ricky) Allen of the Alabama State Mass Choir once sang:

It's only temporary

What you are going through God knows about

71

your problems And He knows just what to do. If you would only trust Him And just take Him at His word.

It's only temporary!

He already knows the burdens that you bear.

He already knows the tears that you shed.

He already knows every need in your life.

The message to you is, "It's only temporary!"

It's only temporary

It's only temporary

It's only temporary

It's only temporary, what you're going through.

Your Sorrows, It's only TEMPORARY

Your pain, It's only TEMPORARY

Your Despair, IT'S ONLY TEMPORARY

You Heartache, IT'S ONLY TEMPORARY

Your Fear, It's only TEMPORARY

Your Depression, It's only TEMPORARY

Your Hopelessness, It's only TEMPORARY

Remember God won't let it last too Long. You can make It!

He didn't bring you this far to abandon you. He didn't allow the storm to rise to destroy you. He allowed it to build your faith, birth your purpose, and break everything in you that wasn't like Him.

1. I may be in the middle of a fight - but it's only temporary.

2. I may be waiting on a breakthrough - but it's only temporary.

3. I may be surrounded by fear - but it's only temporary.

God is not finished with your story. What feels like an ending is often just a transition to something new. Sometimes God has to allow the night so that you'll value the morning.

Don't give up. Don't bow out. Don't let this temporary storm talk you into permanent despair.

Lift up your head, child of God.
The night is almost over. The morning is almost here. And joy is already on its way.

Your Declaration Today:

Say it with faith:

"It's only temporary. My tears are temporary. My trials are temporary. My pain is temporary. But my God is eternal, my hope is eternal, and my victory is eternal!"

IT'S YOUR SEASON TO BE BLESSED!

John 5:1-2– *"After this, there was a feast of the Jews; and Jesus went up to Jerusalem. Now there is at Jerusalem by the sheep market a pool, which is called in the Hebrew tongue Bethesda, having five porches..."*

We are in a season where God is positioning His people for blessings. It's not just a general time of favor; it's your time, your moment, your season. You've endured your night, you've fought your battles, you've sown in tears, now it's time to reap in joy. It's your season to be blessed!

At the pool of Bethesda, there were multitudes of people lying in wait, blind, lame, withered, broken, all waiting for the water to be stirred. They weren't gathered by coincidence. They were gathered in hope. They knew that at a certain season, an angel would trouble the water, and healing would be released.

Let that sink in: the angel didn't come all the time, only at a certain season.

The man with the infirmity had been there for thirty-eight years waiting, hoping, watching. He had almost given up, saying, *"I have no man to put me into the water."* But when Jesus stepped onto the scene, the season shifted! Jesus bypassed the troubling of the water and commanded the blessing directly. *"Rise, take up your bed, and walk."*

Some of you have been lying at the edge of your breakthrough, stuck in a holding pattern, watching others receive while wondering when your turn will come. Let me declare over you today: Your season has arrived! You're not just waiting for a miracle; you are walking into one.

Jesus didn't just heal the man; He changed his entire circumstance. And likewise, God is not finished with you. You are already blessed because you belong to God, but there are commanded blessings coming your way, blessings that will overtake you because of divine timing and obedience.

The Beatitudes in Matthew 5 remind us that we are blessed in ways that go beyond material wealth. God blesses:

1. The humble

2. The grieving

3. The hungry for righteousness

4. The pure in heart

5. The merciful

6. The persecuted

7. The peacemakers

Matthew 5:1-11- And seeing the multitudes, he went up into a mountain: and when he was set, his disciples came unto him:

[2] And he opened his mouth, and taught them, saying,

[3] Blessed are the poor in spirit: for theirs is the kingdom of heaven.

[4] Blessed are they that mourn: for they shall be comforted. [5] Blessed are the meek: for they shall inherit the earth.

[6] Blessed are they which do hunger and thirst after righteousness: for they shall be filled.

[7] Blessed are the merciful: for they shall obtain mercy.

[8] Blessed are the pure in heart: for they shall see God.

[9] Blessed are the peacemakers: for they shall be called the children of God.

[10] Blessed are they which are persecuted for righteousness' sake: for theirs is the kingdom of heaven.

[11]Blessed are ye, when men shall revile you, and persecute you, and shall say all manner of evil against you falsely, for my sake.

In the text, John 5, the Bible says, *"After this there was a feast of the Jews; and Jesus went up to Jerusalem."* It was during this appointed feast that Jesus encountered a multitude gathered at the Pool of Bethesda, located near the Sheep Gate and surrounded by five porches. There lay a multitude of impotent people, those who were blind, lame, paralyzed, all waiting for one thing: the troubling of the water.

We often focus on the miracle that happened to one man that day, the man who had suffered for thirty-eight years, and how Jesus healed him. But what we sometimes overlook is *why* people were getting healed at this pool in the first place. The Scripture tells us that at a certain season, an angel would descend and trouble the waters, and whoever stepped in first was made whole.

This wasn't just an ordinary day. It was an appointed time, a season ordained by God. And these seasons are not random; they are spiritually significant. The Feast of Jehovah mentioned in the text was one of those divine, sacred times. These were not just holidays or religious traditions. They were God's appointed times, divine portals in the calendar when Heaven touches Earth, and supernatural things are released: healing, deliverance, blessing, and breakthrough.

The Feasts of the Lord were set by God Himself. In Leviticus 23, the Lord calls them *"My feasts"*, not Israel's feasts. These were set times or, as the Hebrew calls them, *moedim*, which means appointed times. During these appointed times, the atmosphere was spiritually charged. The heavens were open, and God released something special to those who honored His timing.

So, when Jesus showed up during one of these feast times in John 5, it wasn't a coincidence. The timing was intentional. God was moving, and the angel troubling the water was a sign that a portal had opened. Whoever discerned the moment and responded by stepping into the water was healed instantly.

Let that sink in: It wasn't about the person, their qualifications, or their status. It was about timing and obedience.

John 5:4 tells us:

"For an angel went down at a certain season into the pool and troubled the water: whosoever then first after the

troubling of the water stepped in was made whole of whatsoever disease he had."

The angel stirred the waters at a set time, and only those who moved with the moment received the miracle. Beloved, God is troubling the waters again. The season has shifted. A new window has opened. Heaven is leaning toward Earth, and it's your moment to step in and receive everything God has prepared for you.

"It's your season!"

You may have asked the Lord, *"How long, God?"* You may have waited for years like the man at Bethesda, watching others get their breakthrough while you sat in the same condition. But I declare to you now, the time has come. It's your season to be blessed!

Declare It: My Time Is Now!

1. It's your time to be healed

2. It's your time to be delivered

3. It's your time to be set free

4. It's your time to be raised up

5. It's your time to walk in liberty

6. It's your time to be changed

The waters are moving. The Spirit is stirring. The angel has troubled the water, and God is calling you to move.

What God Is Getting Ready to Do in Your Life:

1. Bring back the broken pieces

2. Heal old and deep wounds

3. Take away the hidden pain

4. Fill the emptiness within you

5. Mend your broken heart

6. Renew your mind and thinking

7. Restore your soul with peace and purpose

But don't miss this truth: Just because it's your season doesn't mean you will automatically receive the blessing.

You have to position yourself to be blessed.

Blessings require positioning. You must be in alignment with God's will to receive what He is releasing.

Too many people want the promise without the process, the gift without the grind, the miracle without the movement. But the man in John 5 had to rise, take up his bed, and walk. That means he had to obey the voice of Jesus, even when it seemed impossible.

We must:

1. Live holy

2. Walk uprightly

3. Pray continually

4. Fast intentionally

5. Remain in the Word

6. Repent quickly

7. Believe fully

You can't continue in sin, dishonor, doubt, or disobedience and expect to step into divine blessing. But when your life lines up with God's heart, nothing can stop the blessing that's been assigned to your season!

WITH THE HELP OF THE LORD

Psalm 46:1 declares, *"God is our refuge and strength, a very present help in trouble."* What a powerful reminder of who God is in our lives. When life becomes overwhelming and we feel like we are drowning in situations beyond our control, the Word of God assures us that He is "a very present help", not a distant helper, not a delayed responder, but an ever-present God right in the midst of our trouble.

Psalm 46:7 reinforces this truth: *"The LORD of hosts is with us; the God of Jacob is our refuge."* Again, in verse 11, the same statement is repeated. Anytime Scripture repeats something, it's not by accident—it's divine emphasis. God wants us to know beyond a shadow of a doubt that He is with us! In chaos, in conflict, in confusion, and in calamity, He is with us.

We all need help sometimes. You can be strong, independent, and capable, but there will always come a time when life presses hard enough that you will need someone bigger than you. The songwriter said, "No man is an island, no man stands alone." Even the strongest need a shoulder to lean on, and we have one in our Heavenly Father.

Psalm 46 paints a picture of global unrest where the nations rage, kingdoms shake, mountains are cast into the sea, the waters roar and foam, but the Psalmist declares, *"We will not fear."* Why? Because God is our refuge. He is our safe place. He is our anchor in unstable waters. Your life may feel shaky. Your future may seem uncertain. But in God, there is stability, peace, and help.

The Psalm concludes with a simple but

commanding truth:

"Be still and know that I am God."

In other words, calm your anxious heart. Rest your worried mind. Settle your troubled spirit. You are not alone, and you are not without help.

When you begin to truly realize that your help does not come from man but from the Lord, you step into a place of spiritual maturity and divine dependency. People often don't recognize their need for help until the situation becomes dire. The truth is, you need help the most when you think you don't. Pride, self-reliance, and independence can blind us to our own desperation.

Most people cry out for help when they run out of options when the bank account is empty, the diagnosis is devastating, or the betrayal is unbearable. But in truth, you needed divine help long before the crisis became visible.

You need the Lord's help when you are:

1. Discouraged

2. Broken

3. Hurting

4. Lonely

5. Sick

6. Depressed

7. Oppressed

8. Lost and wandering

The Lord is not just a helper in times of obvious need. He is a constant support, a present guide, and a faithful comforter.

The word "help" is more than a rescue. It means *to advise, aid, benefit, comfort, guide, support, and assist.*

Remember the man who cried to Jesus: *"Lord, I believe; help thou mine unbelief."* (Mark 9:24) Even in faith, we still need His help to overcome our weakness.

DON'T BECOME WEARY OF THE STRUGGLE

Galatians 6:9 says, *"And let us not be weary in well doing: for in due season, we shall reap, if we faint not."*

The word *weary* means to become tired, exhausted, fatigued, discouraged, bored, or mentally and emotionally worn down. It speaks to the heaviness that weighs on the soul when you've been pressing, praying, and pushing, but nothing seems to be changing. Weariness doesn't always come from doing something wrong; it often comes when you're doing everything right but not seeing the reward. That's why Paul wrote to the Galatians, *Don't be weary in well doing.*

Many believers today are quietly battling behind their smiles. They're showing up, serving, raising families, working two jobs, praying, fasting, but behind closed doors, they are tired. Not just physically tired, but spiritually and emotionally drained.

Single women with children are among the most fatigued in today's world. They are wearing multiple hats. Mother, father, provider, protector, and spiritual leader. They are making critical decisions with no one to lean on, and over time, the stress accumulates. The enemy whispers lies like: *"If you had a man, if you had a sugar daddy, if you just compromised a little, life wouldn't be this hard."* But that's the deception of the enemy; he wants to exhaust you to the point of giving in.

There are people who have remained faithful to low-paying jobs, working hard, being dependable, yet feeling overlooked and underappreciated. Promotions pass them by.

Raises are minimal. Dreams of advancement remain just out of reach. They pray for something better, but the door hasn't opened yet. Weariness creeps in like a slow fog.

There are married couples who are barely holding on. Some spouses feel trapped in routine, in disappointment, in cold silence. They've tried to fix it, tried counseling, tried rekindling the fire, but it feels like nothing changes. That's when weariness sets in—not because they don't love, but because they've grown tired of struggling alone in a union meant for two.

What Is a Struggle?

Struggle is defined as to contest, to battle, to oppose, to clash. It's the internal and external fight against what is holding you back. Struggle exists when two opposing forces are fighting for control. It is the space between where you are and where God is taking you.

But here's the truth: struggle is not a sign of failure. It's a sign that you are still in the fight! The enemy doesn't bother with what isn't a threat. If you're struggling, it's because you're still resisting the enemy's plan for your life.

Let's look at 1 Kings 19:4: *"But he himself went a day's journey into the wilderness, and came and sat down under a juniper tree: and he requested for himself that he might die; and said, It is enough; now, O LORD, take away my life; for I am not better than my fathers."*

Elijah, the mighty prophet of God, who had just called fire down from heaven and destroyed 450 prophets of Baal, found himself weary. Jezebel threatened his life, and he ran. He was exhausted, emotionally drained, and spiritually depleted. He wanted to die. He sat under a tree and said, "It is enough."

Even great men and women of God can get tired. They can have moments where the weight of ministry, life, and struggle feels unbearable. Elijah was not weak; he was weary. There's a difference. Weakness is inability. Weariness is depletion. And God responded. Not with anger, but with restoration. He sent an angel to feed him, to strengthen him, and told him to *"go in the strength of that meat."*

Ephesians 6:12 reminds us: *"For we wrestle not against flesh and blood, but against principalities, against powers, against the rulers of the darkness of this world, against spiritual wickedness in high places."*

This battle isn't just emotional, it's spiritual. Your weariness is not just from your job, your marriage, your kids, or your finances. There is a spiritual war being waged against your faith, your future, and your destiny. The struggle is not against people. It's against principalities. It's a clash between darkness and light. And weariness is the enemy's weapon to make you quit before your breakthrough.

But the good news is found in Isaiah 40:31: *"But they that wait upon the LORD shall renew their strength; they shall mount up with wings as eagles; they shall run, and not be weary; and they shall walk, and not faint."*

God promises to renew your strength if you wait on Him. Waiting doesn't mean sitting still. It means continuing to trust, to serve, to pray, even when nothing looks like it's changing. And while you're waiting, God is working.

There is a renewal coming to your spirit. There is strength on the way. God is about to revive every dry place in your life. Where you've been weary, God is releasing new energy, new focus, and a fresh wind of purpose.

There is a spirit of weariness that has crept into the body of Christ. Saints who once stood strong through storms and battles now find themselves buckling under the pressure. They are tired. Tired of going through financially, struggling to make ends meet, while bills keep piling up. Tired of going through physically, as sickness, fatigue, and weakness attack their bodies day after day. Tired of going through mentally, dealing with anxiety, overthinking, depression, and the never-ending weight of emotional burdens.

There was a time when the people of God were known for resilience. They could take the attacks of the enemy and still declare, *"Though He slay me, yet will I trust Him."* But now, many saints say, *"I don't know how much more I can take. I'm ready to give up."*

That's why we must be reminded of Galatians 6:9 again: *"And let us not be weary in well doing: for in due season we shall reap, if we faint not."* The struggle is real, but so is the promise. The pressure is intense, but the harvest is coming. In the last days, the tests and trials have intensified. The enemy knows his time is short, and he has turned up the heat on every front.

Jude 3 urges us, *"...ye should earnestly contend for the faith which was once delivered unto the saints."* That word *"contend"* means to fight, wrestle, or strive. We're not just holding onto a belief; we're in a fight for our faith. This isn't a season to be passive or casual about your walk with God. You have to fight through fatigue, battle through discouragement, and press through doubt.

It's not enough to say you believe, you've got to keep believing when everything in your life contradicts the promise. Fight for your mind. Fight for your joy. Fight for your marriage. Fight for your children. Fight for your purpose.

In 2 Thessalonians 2:2–3, Paul writes, *"That ye be not soon shaken in mind, or be troubled… Let no man deceive you by any means: for that day shall not come, except there come a falling away first…"*

We're living in that time of falling away. People are abandoning their faith, leaving churches, and walking away from their assignments. Why? Because they've grown weary. Shaken in mind. Troubled in spirit. But God is calling for a remnant that will remain steadfast, unshaken, and rooted.

Don't be moved by every storm or every battle. Anchor yourself in the Word of God. Remind yourself that God is still in control, even when everything around you feels chaotic.

1 Peter 4:12 tells us plainly, *"Beloved, think it not strange concerning the fiery trial which is to try you, as though some strange thing happened unto you."*

The fire you're in is not foreign to God. He allowed it. Not to destroy you but to refine you. Gold must go through the fire to be purified. Diamonds must go through pressure to shine. And saints must go through a struggle to gain strength, endurance, and spiritual maturity.

Don't be shocked by your trial. Expect the resistance. Anticipate the pressure. And know that God is going to bring you through it and not leave you in it.

Romans 7:23–24 captures the internal battle many are facing: *"But I see another law in my members, warring against the law of my mind... O wretched man that I am! Who shall deliver me from the body of this death?"*

Paul describes the war between flesh and spirit. The part of us that wants to do right, serve God, walk in holiness… but also the part of us that's tired, tempted, and wants to quit. The truth is, some of your greatest struggles are not external; they're internal. The enemy knows that if he can weaken your mind, he can stop your progress.

But thank God the battle is not yours, it belongs to the Lord! The very next verse in Romans 7:25 declares, *"I thank God through Jesus Christ our Lord…"* He is our strength. He is our deliverer. And He will pull you out of whatever you're wrestling with.

Let us not forget Jacob, who wrestled with the angel all night. He said, *"I will not let you go until you bless me."* Jacob was weary, but he refused to let go. He was wounded, but he held on. That's the kind of tenacity you need in this season.

You may be limping. You may be broken. But if you refuse to let go of God, the blessing will come.

It's time to bind the spirit of weariness. It's time to speak life back into your situation.

Say aloud:

1. I shall not faint.

2. I shall not quit.

3. I shall not break.

4. I shall not give up.

You are closer to your *due season* than you think. The enemy wants you to walk away just before the harvest, but God says, *"If you faint not, you shall reap."*

To the weary mom, your labor is not in vain.

To the tired pastor, your preaching is not in vain.

To the frustrated worker, your faithfulness is not forgotten.

To the struggling believer, your prayers are not wasted.

To the lonely heart, God has not abandoned you.

You're still in the fight. And that means you're still victorious. The Lord sees your tears. He hears your prayers. And He promises that your weariness will turn into *reaping* if you just hold on a little longer.

The struggle may be real, but so is the strength God gives.

Don't become weary of the struggle. The reward is on the other side.

GOD WILL RESTORE

Joel 2:25– *"And I will restore to you the years that the locust hath eaten..."*

One of the most powerful promises in Scripture is this: *God will restore.* The word "restore" means to bring back, to make new, to replenish, to heal what was broken, to return what was lost, and sometimes, to give even better than what was taken. Many of us have walked through seasons where it felt like the enemy devoured our time, our joy, our finances, our opportunities, or even our relationships. But God says, "I will restore."

Sometimes restoration doesn't come the way we expect. We look for God to give us back exactly what we lost, but often, He gives us something better, something eternal. Maybe you lost years in addiction, pain, confusion, or rebellion. God is not limited by your past. In fact, He specializes in turning your losses into testimonies.

Psalm 71:20-21 says, *"Though you have made me see troubles, many and bitter, you will restore my life again; from the depths of the earth you will again bring me up. You will increase my honor and comfort me once more."*

This is not just a vague hope. It's a divine guarantee. Even after Job lost everything, his wealth, his family, and his health, God restored him. And the Bible says in Job 42:10, *"The Lord gave Job twice as much as he had before."*

Restoration may not always be immediate. There may be a process, a season of healing, pruning, or waiting. But know this: God is never idle. While you're waiting, He's working. While you're broken, He's rebuilding. While you're weeping, He's gathering your tears and preparing your joy.

You may feel like your life has been shattered

into pieces. But in God's hands, broken pieces become a mosaic of grace and glory. The devil comes to steal, kill, and destroy, but Jesus says in John 10:10, *"I am come that they might have life, and have it more abundantly."*

PRAYER IS KEY

Luke 18:1– *"Then Jesus told his disciples a parable to show them that they should always pray and not give up."*

Prayer is not just something we just do; it is the key that unlocks heaven's power. It's the access point between earth and heaven. Prayer isn't a last resort; it's our first response. When we don't know what to do, we pray. When we do know what to do, we still pray. Why? Because prayer invites God into every situation. It acknowledges our dependence on Him and reminds us that He is greater than anything we face.

Many believers underestimate the power of prayer. We treat it like a duty, when in truth, it's a lifeline. Prayer is how we talk to God. But more than that, it's how we connect to His heart. It is both conversation and communion.

James 5:16 tells us, *"The effective, fervent prayer of a righteous man availeth much."* This means your prayers have power. They are not empty words. They move the hand of God. They shift atmospheres. They tear down strongholds. They bring peace to troubled minds and healing to broken bodies. When you pray, heaven listens.

Prayer changes things, but it also changes you. It shifts your perspective, strengthens your spirit, and aligns your heart with God's will. Sometimes, prayer doesn't change the situation immediately, but it changes you to handle the situation with grace and wisdom.

In Philippians 4:6-7, Paul writes, *"Do not be anxious about anything, but in everything, by prayer and petition, with thanksgiving, present your requests to God. And the peace of God… will guard your hearts and your minds in Christ Jesus."*

Prayer brings peace. Peace that surpasses understanding. Peace that holds you together when everything is falling apart. Peace that tells your heart: *God is in control.*

When you face confusion, prayer is your compass. When you face trials, prayer is your shield. When you face decisions, prayer is your guide.

We often say, "All I can do is pray," as if prayer is weak. But the truth is prayer is the most powerful thing you can do. Heaven responds to a praying heart. Angels are released when you pray. Miracles are born through prayer. Chains are broken, doors are opened, battles are won because someone decided to kneel before God.

Jesus Himself often withdrew to pray. If the Son of God needed prayer, how much more do we?

Mark 1:35 tells us, *"Very early in the morning, while*

it was still dark, Jesus got up, left the house and went off to a solitary place, where he prayed."

Don't wait until you're desperate. Don't wait until you're overwhelmed. Make prayer your lifestyle, not your emergency line. Begin your day with prayer. End your day with prayer. Saturate your decisions, your family, your future, and your heart in prayer.

Prayer is not complicated. You don't need fancy words, just a sincere heart. He hears you in the whisper. He sees your tears. He knows the words you cannot say.

So, pray in the valley. Pray on the mountain. Pray in faith. Pray when it hurts. Pray when you're full of joy.

Because prayer is key. And when you hold the key, no door is truly locked.

YOU'RE COMING OUT OF LODEBAR

2 Samuel 9:5 – *"Then King David sent and brought him out of the house of Machir the son of Ammiel, from Lodebar."*

Lodebar means "no pasture," a place of barrenness, isolation, and shame. It was where Mephibosheth was crippled, forgotten, fearful and was hiding. Once the grandson of a king, now he was living in obscurity. But one day, everything changed. King David called for him not to punish him, but to restore him. And in that moment, Mephibosheth's story shifted.

You may be in your own Lodebar right now. A place where you feel forgotten, broken, or unworthy. Maybe life has wounded you. Maybe you've been dropped, like Mephibosheth, by someone you trusted. Maybe your dreams feel dead, and your heart is weary. But the word of the Lord to you today is you are coming out of Lodebar.

God has not forgotten you. Heaven knows your name. The same God who stirred David's heart to remember Mephibosheth is stirring things on your behalf. Doors are about to open. Favor is about to locate you. You're not going to die in that dry place. God is calling you higher, calling you out, calling you home.

Mephibosheth didn't earn the invitation. It came because of a covenant David had made with Jonathan, his father. In the same way, your breakthrough is not based on your performance but on God's covenant of mercy and grace through Jesus Christ. Because of the cross, you have been chosen, forgiven, redeemed, and remembered.

Lodebar was not his final destination, and it is not yours either.

David didn't just bring Mephibosheth out; he restored him. He gave him a seat at the royal table. He gave him servants, land, and a new identity. The boy who once hid in shame now ate at the king's table as a son.

That's what God wants to do for you. Not just pull you out, but restore what was lost. Heal what was broken. Elevate what was overlooked.

You're coming out of hiding. Out of depression. Out of rejection. Out of fear. Out of low self-worth. Out of survival mode. God is not only calling you out. He's calling you up.

Isaiah 61:7 says, *"Instead of your shame you shall receive double honor..."* That is your promise. Your season in Lodebar was real, but it was never meant to last forever. It was preparation for elevation. It built resilience. It deepened your faith. And now, it's time to rise.

You may walk with a limp, like Mephibosheth. Your scars may still be there. But they do not disqualify you. In fact, they are a testimony of survival and grace.

So, lift your head. The King has sent for you. His grace is greater than your shame. His love is stronger than your past. Your seat at the table is ready.

You're coming out of Lodebar and you're stepping into restoration, identity, and honor.

DON'T GIVE UP NOW

Galatians 6:9– *"And let us not be weary in well doing: for in due season we shall reap, if we faint not."*

You've come too far to give up now.

It's easy to feel weary when the prayers seem unanswered, the doors stay shut, and the promises feel delayed. Life has a way of testing your endurance just before the breakthrough. But the truth is, right when you're about to quit is often when you're closest to the miracle.

The enemy loves to whisper, "It's not worth it. Nothing is changing. You'll never make it." But those are lies meant to derail you from your destiny. If God started a good work in you, He will complete it. (*Philippians 1:6*)

The pain you're facing is not a sign of

abandonment; it's a sign of *birth*. Every mother knows that the greatest pain comes right before delivery. In the same way, your spiritual contractions are intensifying because something new is about to be born in your life. Don't walk away from the promise just because you're tired.

Sometimes the silence of God makes us question His presence. But silence is not absence. He's still working behind the scenes, orchestrating what you cannot see. Keep praying even when you feel nothing. Keep worshipping even when you don't understand. Heaven hears.

You may have failed. You may feel unqualified. You may be battling depression, shame, or fear. But you are not a mistake. God chose you, knowing every flaw. Your struggle does not disqualify you; it proves you're still fighting. You are stronger than you think, because God's strength is made perfect in your weakness. (*2 Corinthians 12:9*).

Don't give up on the vision.

If God gave you the dream, He will give you the provision. The doors will open in His timing. The right people will come. The opportunities will align. But sometimes He allows the waiting to grow your faith, to prepare your character, and to deepen your trust.

What if today is the day everything starts to change?

What if the breakthrough is just on the other side of your next step of obedience?

What if your story will inspire someone else not to give up?

You never know how close you are to the finish line. That's why you can't afford to stop now.

Hold on to the promises. Hold on to your identity. Hold on to your worship. Hold on to the Word. Even when your hands are trembling, even when your heart is heavy, hold on.

Hebrews 10:23 says, *"Let us hold fast the profession of our faith without wavering; (for he is faithful that promised)."*

He is faithful.

You may cry, but don't quit. You may crawl, but don't stop. You may stumble, but keep going. God is still with you. The night may feel long, but morning is coming. (*Psalm 30:5*) And with it joy, strength, and new hope.

So, don't give up now.

Your harvest is near.

Your healing is near.

Your help is near.

Keep going for God's not done with you yet.

THE STRUGGLE IS OVER

Isaiah 43:18-19– *"Remember ye not the former things, neither consider the things of old. Behold, I will do a new thing; now it shall spring forth; shall ye not know it?"*

For too long, you've cried. For too long, you've wrestled silently with battles that nobody else could see. You've smiled in public and wept in private. You've prayed through the night, asking God when the struggle will end. And now, He's whispering into your heart that the struggle is over."

There comes a moment in every believer's journey when God draws the line. A moment when heaven declares an end to suffering and the beginning of peace. That moment is now. The same God who delivered the Israelites from Egypt, who shut the mouths of lions for Daniel, and who calmed the storm for the disciples is saying to you, *"I've seen your affliction, and I'm stepping in."*

The enemy may have tried to convince you that this is your permanent state. That the financial hardship, the depression, the broken relationship, the delayed promise, or the barren place will always be your portion. But God has not forgotten you. In fact, it's often when we feel the most forsaken that God is closest. He specializes in turning mourning into dancing, ashes into beauty, and valleys into victory.

When Jesus declared on the cross, *"It is finished,"* He wasn't just talking about His mission. He was also talking about every curse, every chain, every struggle that would try to weigh down His children. Through His finished work, you now have access to peace, restoration, healing, and breakthrough.

Yes, you may have struggled in your mind, tormented by anxiety, haunted by failure, but the struggle is over. Your thoughts are aligning with the truth. Your heart is being renewed. The weight is lifting. God is giving you rest.

Yes, you may have struggled in your relationships, constantly misunderstood, rejected, or betrayed. But the struggle is over. God is bringing the right people into your life, healing old wounds, and restoring your confidence in love.

Yes, you may have struggled financially, working hard with little to show. But the struggle is over. God is releasing provision, wisdom, and divine opportunities to establish you in abundance.

This is not to say you will never face challenges again, but there's a difference between a battle and a burden. The burden that pressed you down, that made you feel like giving up, that burden is being lifted by the hand of God.

Take a moment to breathe. Not just with your lungs, but with your spirit. Let peace return. Let hope rise. Let the Word of God wash over you and remind you of who you are: not a victim of struggle, but a vessel of victory.

Joel 2:25 declares, *"And I will restore to you the years that the locust hath eaten…"* The struggle has stolen enough time, joy, and confidence. But restoration is here.

Walk in it. Speak it. Believe it.

The struggle is over, not because of your strength, but because of His promise.

I AM A SURVIVOR

2 Corinthians 4:8–9– *"We are troubled on every side, yet not distressed; we are perplexed, but not in despair; persecuted, but not forsaken; cast down, but not destroyed."*

In Christ, we are survivors not by human effort, but by divine empowerment. The believer's life is not without battles, trials, or suffering. In fact, to follow Christ is to endure hardship, carry the cross, and stand firm against spiritual opposition. Yet in the midst of all these, Scripture reminds us that we are *not destroyed*. We survive because He sustains.

A survivor in Christ is one who endures not by might, nor by power, but by the Spirit of the living God (Zechariah 4:6). No matter what comes. Temptation, affliction, spiritual warfare, betrayal, or delay, the believer stands, not in their own strength, but in the finished work of the cross. We are alive today not just physically, but spiritually, because Christ lives in us.

To survive in Christ means to remain rooted and unshaken in faith even when the winds of life blow fiercely. Like the house built upon the rock in Matthew 7:24–25, the rain descended, the floods came, and the winds blew and beat upon that house, but it did not fall, because it was founded on the Rock. Christ is our Rock. Our survival is not random; it is anchored in the unshakable foundation of the Word.

Believers are not exempt from sorrow or persecution. Paul, in 2 Corinthians 11, listed the many hardships he suffered: stripes, imprisonments, shipwrecks, hunger, danger, and more. Yet through it all, he pressed on, because his hope was in Christ. Survival in Christ is not mere endurance; it is the triumph of grace over adversity, the assurance that *nothing can separate us from the love of God* (Romans 8:38–39).

We are survivors because Christ has overcome the world. *"In the world ye shall have tribulation: but be of good cheer; I have overcome the world"* (John 16:33). Because He overcame, we too overcome. Our survival is not about escaping the battle, but emerging from it with faith intact, testimony secured, and Christ glorified.

To be in Christ is to survive sin, shame, condemnation, and eternal separation from God. We were once dead in trespasses, but now we live by the Spirit. We have passed from death to life (John 5:24). This is the greatest survival. The salvation of our souls.

Therefore, let the redeemed of the Lord say so.

We are survivors not because the storm didn't come, but because our God is greater than the storm. We are more than conquerors through Him who loved us (Romans 8:37). This is our identity. This is our victory.

Let every believer boldly declare: *"I am a survivor in Christ. I have endured by grace. I stand by faith. I live by His power. And I will continue to overcome through Him who strengthens me."*

SPIRITUAL WARFARE

Ephesians 6:12 (KJV) *"For we wrestle not against flesh and blood, but against principalities, against powers, against the rulers of the darkness of this world, against spiritual wickedness in high places."*

Spiritual warfare is real. Every believer is engaged in a battle that cannot be seen with the natural eye. This is not a physical fight, but a spiritual one. A war waged in the unseen realm between the kingdom of light and the kingdom of darkness. To ignore this reality is to live vulnerable, unguarded, and unprepared.

The enemy, Satan, is a deceiver, accuser, and tempter. His goal is to steal, kill, and destroy (John 10:10). He attacks through fear, discouragement, doubt, temptation, and lies. He knows he cannot take your salvation, but he seeks to rob your peace, weaken your faith, and render you ineffective in your walk with God.

But thanks be to God, we are not left defenseless. The Lord has equipped us with everything we need to stand and fight. Ephesians 6:13–17 outlines the whole armor of God:

1. The belt of truth, which holds all things together and counters the enemy's lies.

2. The breastplate of righteousness, protecting our hearts and reminding us we are made right with God through Christ.

3. The gospel of peace on our feet, giving us stability and readiness in the face of chaos.

4. The shield of faith, able to quench all the fiery darts of the wicked.

5. The helmet of salvation, guarding our minds from confusion and despair.

6. The sword of the Spirit, which is the Word of God—our only offensive weapon.

Prayer is also essential in spiritual warfare. Ephesians 6:18 commands us to pray always with all kinds of prayer and supplication. When we pray, we reinforce our position in the Spirit. We declare God's will and resist the enemy's influence. Jesus Himself said, "Watch and pray, that ye enter not into temptation" (Matthew 26:41). A prayerless believer is an easy target.

Spiritual warfare also involves resistance. *"Resist the devil, and he will flee from you"* (James 4:7). Resistance begins with submission to God. You cannot overcome what you continually entertain. To resist is to reject sin, deny the flesh, and stand firm in God's truth.

Remember, the battle is already won. Christ disarmed principalities and powers through His death and resurrection (Colossians 2:15). We do not fight for victory; we fight from victory. Our position is seated with Christ in heavenly places (Ephesians 2:6), far above every demonic influence.

So, don't live in fear. Walk in authority. Take up your armor daily. Pray without ceasing. Speak the Word boldly. Bind and loose in Jesus' name. And stand firm, knowing that greater is He who is in you than he who is in the world (1 John 4:4).

You are not alone. Heaven backs you. Angels surround you. Christ fights for you. The battle belongs to the Lord, and in Him, you are more than a conqueror.

OVERDUE

Ecclesiastes 3:1 (KJV) *"To every thing there is a season, and a time to every purpose under the heaven."*

Have you ever felt like the breakthrough should have come by now? Like the answer to your prayer is long overdue? Maybe you've been waiting on healing, provision, promotion, deliverance, or restoration. You've done all you know to do. You have prayed, fasted, trusted, obeyed and still, it feels like heaven is silent. You begin to wonder, *Did God forget me?* But hear this clearly: what God has for you is not denied, it is simply delayed until the appointed time.

God does not operate on our calendar. His timing is perfect, even when it seems late. Think of Abraham and Sarah; they waited 25 years for a promised child. Or Joseph, who had a divine dream but endured betrayal, slavery, and prison before it was fulfilled. What God ordained for them seemed long overdue by human standards, but it came to pass right on time in heaven's agenda.

Delay does not mean denial. Sometimes God uses the wait to prepare you for what He has prepared for you. He strengthens your faith, refines your character, teaches you endurance, and strips away pride and self-dependence. He stretches your trust so that when the blessing arrives, you know without a doubt—it was the hand of God and not your own efforts.

Galatians 6:9 reminds us: *"And let us not be weary in well doing: for in due season we shall reap, if we faint not."* The key is *due season*. There is a set time for every promise to manifest. And if you don't give up, if you continue to believe, you will reap.

Sometimes, what's overdue is not just for you it's connected to others. God may delay a thing because He's aligning people, places, and conditions for a bigger impact. What feels like a personal delay may actually be divine coordination. Remember Lazarus? Jesus delayed going to him until he had died. It wasn't neglect, it was intentional. Because when Jesus raised him from the dead, it became a testimony that brought glory to God. What looked overdue was actually setting the stage for a miracle.

And don't forget the widow in Luke 18, who kept coming to the unjust judge for justice. She didn't stop knocking, and eventually, she got what was hers. Jesus used that parable to encourage us to keep praying and not give up. If an unjust judge can respond to persistence, how much more will our righteous and loving Father?

You may feel like you're on the verge of giving up, but don't. What you've been praying for is not lost. What you've sown in tears, you will reap in joy. The doors you've knocked on will open. The promises you've held on to will come to pass. Your testimony is overdue by your measure but right on time by God's.

So, hold on, beloved. Your overdue season is turning into a right now season. The wait is ending. The heavens are moving. The rain is coming. When it comes, it will be pressed down, shaken together, and running over.

God is never late. He's just setting the stage. And your due date is here.

THE MAKING OF A CHAMPION

2 Timothy 2:3–5 (KJV): *"Thou therefore endure hardness, as a good soldier of Jesus Christ... And if a man also strive for masteries, yet is he not crowned, except he strive lawfully."*

Champions aren't born; they are made. They are shaped in hidden places, forged in fire, and strengthened through trials. A champion is not simply one who wins a battle but one who has been trained, tested, and tempered by the hand of God to overcome every battle.

In the kingdom of God, a champion is someone who stands tall not by strength alone, but by faith. Champions are not made on the stage, but in the shadows, in prayer closets, in wilderness seasons, in the furnace of affliction, and in the school of obedience. Just like David, Joseph, Esther, and Paul, every true champion in Christ has a process in his making.

Let us explore what it means to be made a champion in Christ.

1. **Champions Are Formed in Obscurity**

Before David defeated Goliath publicly, he had already conquered the lion and the bear in secret. While others overlooked him, God was preparing him. No applause, no recognition, no spotlight. just faithfulness in the field. Sometimes God hides you to prepare you. He trains your hands for war when no one is watching. That job you hate, that family struggle, that dry season, they are your training ground.

God uses obscurity to humble us, to strip us of pride, and to teach us to depend on Him.

He doesn't rush the process. He develops champions slowly so that when they finally emerge, they carry not only victory but also character.

2. Champions Endure Hardships

Champions are not exempt from suffering; in fact, suffering is part of the curriculum. 2 Timothy 2:3 says, "Endure hardness, as a good soldier of Jesus Christ." The path to victory is often paved with tears, rejection, loss, and pain. But these challenges are not designed to break you; they are designed to build you.

Joseph was thrown into a pit, sold as a slave, falsely accused, and imprisoned before he ever sat on the throne. His trials did not disqualify him; they qualified him. Each step was part of the making. Had he not gone through the pit, he wouldn't have had the compassion and wisdom to rule Egypt.

Pain, in the hands of God, becomes purpose. The fire you are going through is not to consume you but to refine you like gold.

3. **Champions Are Disciplined**

Champions don't live like everyone else. They deny themselves to gain something greater. Just like an athlete trains and says no to distractions, a spiritual champion disciplines their thoughts, appetites, and actions. 1 Corinthians 9:24-27 says Paul disciplined his body like an athlete to win the prize. Champions fast, pray, study the Word, walk in integrity, even when it's uncomfortable.

God cannot trust a person who lacks discipline with lasting victory. The making of a champion involves learning self-control, resisting temptation, and being consistent in the small things.

4. **Champions Learn to Fight with God's Weapons**

You don't become a champion by fighting in the flesh. You win by using the weapons God has given you: faith, prayer, the Word, righteousness, truth, and praise. David could not fight Goliath in Saul's armor. He had to use what God gave him: a sling, five stones, and the name of the Lord.

Champions know how to go to war in the Spirit. They fight not with fists, but with faith. Not with fear, but with the sword of the Word. They understand that *"the weapons of our warfare are not carnal, but mighty through God to the pulling down of strongholds"* (2 Corinthians 10:4).

5. **Champions Stay Humble**

True champions give glory to God. They know they didn't make it by their own power. After David defeated Goliath, he didn't exalt himself; he exalted God. Champions don't seek attention; they seek God's approval. They serve others, love deeply, and live for something greater than themselves.

Pride disqualifies, but humility sustains. God lifts the humble and uses them mightily. Champions are not perfect, but they are surrendered. They recognize their weaknesses and lean on God's strength.

6. **Champions Inspire Others**

Champions don't just fight for themselves. They fight for nations, for families, for the lost. When David killed Goliath, the entire nation of Israel rose in courage. Champions spark revival. They are vessels through which others are healed, restored, and empowered.

You are not being made just for yourself. Your process is preparing you to lift others. Your testimony will be someone's survival guide.

The making of a champion is not easy, but it is worth it. You are being trained, tested, and transformed for greater things. Don't despise the process. Embrace the pruning. Stay faithful in the wilderness. Keep praying, keep believing, keep standing. God is shaping you into a vessel of honor, a warrior for His kingdom, and a voice in this generation.

You are not defeated. You are in training. And soon, the world will see the masterpiece God has been working on all along.

You are being made into a champion.

ABOUT THE AUTHOR

Dr. Frank L. Hammonds is a seasoned servant of the Lord with over five decades of faithful ministry. He preached his first sermon at just 13 years old and was ordained as minister by Bishop C.E. Bennett. In 1981, he was ordained as an Elder by Bishop William O. Blakely. That same year, he married his beloved wife, with whom he shares one daughter, born in 1982.

In 1986, he answered God's call to establish his first church, launching a lifelong apostolic work. Known for his pioneering spirit, Dr. Hammonds has planted and pastored churches across the country and has been a spiritual father to many. In 2002, he was ordained as an Apostle by Apostle John Eckhardt of Chicago, IL, confirming his mantle to build, establish, and strengthen churches from the ground up.

His ministry has taken him across denominational lines and into pulpits across the nation, where he has evangelized with passion, prophetic insight, and deep biblical teaching. Among the many highlights of his journey was the opportunities to minister at Monument of Faith under the leadership of the late Apostle Richard D. Henton of Chicago, IL—moments he cherishes as an honor. He was also profoundly impacted by the late Dr. Myles Munroe, who prayed that the mantle that was on his life; would also be upon Dr. Hammonds.

In 2025, Dr. Hammonds was awarded an honoris causa Doctor of Philosophy in Spiritual Formation by Dr. Gordon E. Bradshaw from the Misrah Academy Governmental

Empowerment Center, recognizing his lifetime of work in discipling, mentoring, and forming champions for the Kingdom.

Apostolic in authority, pastoral in heart, and prophetic in vision, Dr. Hammonds continues to pour into the next generation of leaders, praying that the mantle on his life would fall upon those called to carry the fire forward. Dr. Hammonds is currently the Pastor of Miracles Do Happen Ministries in Denton, TX.

The Making of a Champion is a reflection of his life's message, that true greatness is forged in surrender, obedience, and faithfulness to God's call.